SCIENTIFIC AMERICAN EDUCATIONAL PUBLISHING
MOVE IT!
10 FUN
PHYSICAL SCIENCE PROJECTS WITH VEHICLES
BRING SCIENCE HOME

Published in 2023 by The Rosen Publishing Group, Inc.
2544 Clinton St, Buffalo, NY 14224

First Edition

Editor: Jennifer Lombardo
Designer: Rachel Rising

Activity on page 5 by Science Buddies/Ben Finio (February 6, 2020); page 11 Science Buddies/Ben Finio (November 14, 2020); page 15 by Science Buddies/Ben Finio (October 24, 2019); page 19 by Science Buddies/Svenja Lohner (September 12, 2019); page 25 Science Buddies/Megan Arnett (January 31, 2019); page 31 Science Buddies/Ben Finio (November 1, 2018); page 37 Science Buddies/Ben Finio (January 11, 2018); page 43 Science Buddies/Sabine de Brabandere (December 28, 2017); page 49 Science Buddies/Ben Finio (May 18, 2017); page 55 Science Buddies/Ben Finio (January 26, 2017).

Photo Credits: pp. 4, 5, 11, 15, 19, 25, 31, 37, 43, 49, 55 Anna Frajtova/Shutterstock.com; pp. 4, 5, 8, 11, 13, 14, 15, 18, 19, 22, 25, 28, 31, 34, 37, 41, 43, 46, 47, 49, 52, 55, 58, 59 cve iv/Shutterstock.com.

All illustrations by Continuum Content Solutions

Cataloging-in-Publication Data
Names: Scientific American, inc.
Title: Move it! / edited by the Editors of Scientific American.
Description: Buffalo, New York : Scientific American Educational Publishing, 2023. | Series: Bring science home | Includes glossary and index.
Identifiers: ISBN 9781684169870 (pbk.) | ISBN 9781684169887 (library bound) | ISBN 9781684169894 (ebook)
Subjects: LCSH: Physics--Experiments--Juvenile literature. | Science projects--Juvenile literature.
Classification: LCC QC25.M684 2023 | DDC 530--dc23

Manufactured in the United States of America

Some of the images in this book illustrate individuals who are models. The depictions do not imply actual situations or events.

CPSIA Compliance Information: Batch #SACS23. For further information contact Rosen Publishing at 1-800-237-9932.

CONTENTS

INTRODUCTION

Have you ever wondered how cars, trains, airplanes, and other vehicles move? They all involve physics, and there are a lot of different ways you can use this science. You can experiment with various methods of propulsion and different ways of building vehicles with the physics activities in this book.

Projects marked with ⚛ include a section called Science Fair Ideas. These ideas can help you develop your own original science fair project. Science fair judges tend to reward creative thought and imagination, and it helps if you are really interested in your project. You will also need to follow the scientific method. See pages 61 for more information about that.

Build a Paper Airplane Launcher

FLYING FAST IS A SNAP—WITH A LITTLE BOOST FROM PHYSICS!

PROJECT TIME

60 to 90 minutes

Here's a challenge: Try throwing a paper airplane by moving *just* your wrist (don't move your elbow or shoulder). It's hard, isn't it? How could you get a paper airplane to fly far if you can use only a short distance to launch it? Try this activity to find out!

KEY CONCEPTS

Physics
Speed
Lift
Potential energy
Kinetic energy
Engineering design

BACKGROUND

In order to take off, an airplane has to generate enough lift (upward force due to air pushing on the plane) to overcome its weight (downward force due to gravity). The faster an airplane goes, the more lift it generates. This is why airport runways are usually very long (sometimes longer than 1 mile, or 1.6 km)—because planes need a lot of space to gain enough speed to take off. They also need a lot of space to land safely and slow down from such high speeds.

Aircraft carriers are large ships with runways on them that allow aircraft to take off and land in the open ocean. Although aircraft carriers are huge compared with most other ships, they are very small compared with land-based airports and runways. The largest aircraft carrier is just longer than 1,000 feet (305 m), which is still less than 0.25 mile (0.4 km). Airplanes can't gain enough speed to take off on their own over such a short distance, so they get an extra boost from a type of catapult (not the big wooden kind you might imagine flinging stones at castle walls). This catapult provides extra energy from a source such as compressed air or electromagnets to help the plane gain extra speed. The catapult hooks onto the plane and helps it accelerate over a much shorter distance so that it can get enough speed and lift to take off.

You don't need any compressed air or electromagnets to build your own airplane catapult, however. In this project, you will build one using a rubber band. It stores potential energy, which gives extra kinetic energy (motion energy) to the paper airplane—even over a short distance. It's much more effective than just using your wrist!

MATERIALS

- Paper
- Rubber bands
- Pen or pencil
- Paper clips
- Tape or stapler
- Construction materials to build a paper airplane launcher. You can use whatever materials you have available. Examples include cardboard, building toys such as LEGO® or K'NEX®, or wood.
- Open area to launch paper airplanes (without wind or strong drafts)

PREPARATION

- To do this project, you will need to know how to build a basic paper airplane. If you don't know how to make a paper airplane, instructions are available online and in many books.
- Build several paper airplanes to test. Because paper airplanes can get bent or destroyed easily, it's a good idea to build more than one. Ensure that they are all built the same for this activity.
- Tape or staple a paper clip to the nose of each paper airplane. The outer straight part of the paper clip should point backward, parallel to the bottom of the plane, so it can serve as a hook to attach to the rubber band. There will be some pull on the hook, so make sure it's secure.
- Practice throwing your paper airplane using your entire arm. *How far can you throw your plane? How much do you move your arm when you throw it?*
- Now try to throw your airplane only using your wrist. Keep your shoulder and elbow still. *How far can you throw the plane now?*
- Next, try launching your airplane using a very simple "catapult." Hook one end of a rubber band around the end of a pencil (such as around the metal ring by the eraser). Hook the paper clip on the nose of a plane around the other end of the rubber band, and pull it back to stretch the rubber band. Aim the plane forward, and release. *How far does the plane go now? How far did you have to stretch the rubber band compared to how far you moved your arm or wrist?*

PROCEDURE

- Now use the engineering design process to build a more permanent launcher for your airplane.

- Think about the criteria for your design. You will need to build a device to support the rubber band. It will need to be strong enough that it does not collapse when you pull back on the rubber band. You will also need to make sure the paper airplane does not get caught or snagged on the device when you launch it.
- Draw a few sketches of your design ideas, and pick one to build.
- Build a prototype of your design. You might find that things don't fit together like you thought they would, and you need to change your design. That's okay!
- Test your airplane launcher. It probably won't work perfectly on the first try. *What changes can you make to your design to make it better?*
- Keep improving your launcher and testing it again (and, if necessary, again). This process is called iteration, and designers and engineers use it often in their work. *How does the plane's flight distance compare to when you threw with your arm or with your wrist?*

SCIENCE FAIR IDEA

How does the angle at which you launch the plane affect its flight distance?

SCIENCE FAIR IDEA

Try using different lengths and thicknesses of rubber bands. *Do some work better than others? Why do you think that is?*

OBSERVATIONS AND RESULTS

You probably found that it was very difficult to throw your paper airplane very far when using only your wrist. Your wrist has a much smaller range of motion than your entire arm, and it's difficult to get the airplane going fast enough for a long flight. A rubber band, however, can store quite a bit of energy in a relatively small distance when it is stretched. A launcher built with a rubber band can get the paper airplane going fast over a much shorter distance, allowing you to launch it much farther than you can with just your wrist—possibly even farther than you could with your entire arm!

CLEANUP

Put away the materials you used.

Make a Marble Roller Coaster

LOOP-THE-LOOP WITH A LITTLE PHYSICS! BUILD A MINIATURE ROLLER COASTER, AND SEE IF YOU CAN GET MARBLES TO GO THE DISTANCE—AND UPSIDE-DOWN!

PROJECT TIME

60 to 75 minutes

How much energy does a roller-coaster car need to go through a loop without getting stuck? Build your own marble roller coaster in this project and find out!

KEY CONCEPTS

Physics
Gravity
Potential energy
Kinetic energy
Friction
Conservation of energy

BACKGROUND

Roller coasters rely on two types of energy to operate: gravitational potential energy and kinetic energy. Gravitational potential energy is the energy an object has stored because of its mass and its height off the ground. Kinetic energy is the energy an object has because of its mass and its velocity.

When a roller-coaster car reaches the very top of its first big hill, it has a lot of potential energy because it is very high off the ground. It moves over the top of the hill very slowly, so it has almost no kinetic energy. Then, it drops down the other side of the hill and starts going very fast as its height rapidly decreases. The potential energy is converted to kinetic energy. This process repeats as the car goes through hills, loops, twists, and turns. Whenever it goes up, it gains more potential energy with height but loses kinetic energy as it slows down. Energy is never created or destroyed—it just converts from one form to another. This principle is known as conservation of energy.

We know from experience, however, that a roller coaster doesn't keep going forever. Eventually, it slows down because of friction (a combination of air resistance and contact with the track). If energy isn't created or destroyed, where does that energy go? It is converted into heat. This is why you can rub your hands together to warm them up—friction converts energy from your moving hands into heat!

Does conservation of energy restrict a roller coaster's movement? For example, can a roller coaster ever go through a loop that is taller than its initial hill? Try this project to find out!

MATERIALS

- Foam pipe insulation (1.5 inches, or 4 cm, in diameter and at least 6 feet, or 1.8 m, in length—or more if you plan to add more features to your roller coaster)
- At least one glass marble (or other small heavy ball that will roll easily through the foam insulation, such as a metal ball bearing)
- Masking tape
- Utility knife
- Table or chair
- Adult helper

PREPARATION

- Ask an adult to use the utility knife to cut the pipe insulation in half lengthwise, forming two U-shaped channels.

PROCEDURE

- Curl one end of a piece of pipe insulation into a loop roughly 1 foot (0.3 m) in diameter.
- Use masking tape to hold the loop in place, and tape it to the floor on both sides of the loop. Make sure tape is not blocking the inside of the channel (it's okay to have tape on the inside, just make sure it is pressed flat against the foam and will not block the marble).
- Tape the free end of the pipe insulation to a table or chair, forming a large hill leading down to the loop.
- Place your marble a few inches from the bottom of the hill, and release it. *Does the marble make it through the loop?*
- Move your marble a few inches up the track, and release it again. Keep repeating this process until the marble goes the whole way through the loop. *How high does the starting position need to be before the marble goes through the loop? Is it lower, the same height, or higher than the top of the loop?*
- If you need to make your hill higher, tape the two pieces of pipe insulation together end-to-end, and keep trying from greater heights.
- *Can you describe how energy is changing throughout your marble's journey down the "coaster"?*

SCIENCE FAIR IDEA

Add other features to your roller coaster, such as twists, turns and spirals. *How high does the hill need to be for the marble to make it through all the features without stopping?*

SCIENCE FAIR IDEA

Watch your marble closely, and observe its velocity. *Where is the marble going the fastest? Where is it going the slowest?*

SCIENCE FAIR IDEA

Add a straight piece of track to the end of your roller coaster at the bottom of the loop. *How far does the marble roll before friction brings it to a stop?*

OBSERVATIONS AND RESULTS

You should have found that the marble had to start higher than the top of the loop in order to make it the whole way through the loop. This happens because some energy is always lost to friction as the marble rolls down the track. You need to start the marble higher than the top of the loop so it has enough extra energy to get the whole way through the loop without stopping.

If you watch the marble closely, you might be able to see that it is going the fastest right at the bottom of the hill before it enters the loop. As the marble rolls down the hill, its potential energy is converted to kinetic energy (its height decreases, but its velocity increases). When the marble goes back up the loop, its height increases again and its velocity decreases, changing kinetic energy into potential energy. If you added a straight piece of track at the bottom of your loop, you could observe how the marble gradually rolled to a stop due to friction.

The more features you add to your track, the more initial potential energy the marble will need to make it through all of them without stopping. You might notice that the pipe insulation flexes and bends as the marble zips around—this can also cause the marble to lose some energy (it takes energy to bend the insulation). Making your track more rigid by taping it to supports (such as boxes or pieces of furniture) will help avoid this type of energy loss, allowing your marble to go farther.

CLEANUP

Put away the materials you used.

Build a Wind-Powered Car

GO WITH THE WIND: BUILD A CAR THAT HARNESSES MOVING AIR FOR POWER. DESIGN YOUR OWN EFFICIENT "SAILCAR."

PROJECT TIME

90 to 120 minutes

Is that a sailboat or a sail ... car? Design and build a toy car powered by the wind in this fun engineering project!

KEY CONCEPTS

Physics
Forces
Friction
Engineering

BACKGROUND

You've probably seen a sailboat at some point—but maybe not a "sailcar." Why don't we have more wind-powered cars? Sailboats must zig-zag back and forth if they want to sail directly into the wind. It probably wouldn't be very safe if we had cars zig-zagging all over the road on a windy day! Although it might not be practical to use a sailcar on the road in real life, building a toy one is a fun engineering project.

When moving air pushes on your car's sail, it exerts a force on the sail. This force pushes the car forward. The force, however, must be big enough to overcome any friction in the spinning axles. That friction can be greater if your axles are misaligned or if your wheels are wobbly. You might think you could always make your car go faster by adding a bigger sail. A bigger sail will catch more air, so exert a bigger force, and make the car go faster—right? Not necessarily! A bigger sail is also heavier (it has more mass). It takes more force to move a bigger mass, and a heavier car will also have more friction in its axles. If a sail is too big, it could even make the car so top-heavy that it tips over. What size sail works best? Try this project to find out!

MATERIALS

- Corrugated cardboard
- Construction paper or cardstock
- Three wooden skewers
- Two plastic straws
- Four plastic bottle caps
- Tape
- Scissors
- Hobby knife
- Fan
- Long hallway or large room (smooth floors work best)
- Adult helper

PREPARATION

- Carefully cut out a piece of cardboard to form the body of your car.
- Tape two straws across the bottom of your car, one at each end. Make sure the straws are parallel.

- Have an adult use the hobby knife to carefully poke a "+"-shaped hole in the center of each bottle cap.
- Push a wooden skewer through the hole in one of the bottle caps (and please push it away from your face!).
- Thread the other end of the skewer through one of the straws.
- Push a bottle cap onto the end of the skewer opposite the first bottle cap. You just made an axle with two wheels for your car!
- Repeat these steps to make the other axle.
- Make sure the axles can spin and the car can roll smoothly without getting stuck. If needed, adjust the wheels so they are not too wobbly.
- Have an adult use the hobby knife to carefully poke a small hole in the middle of the cardboard.
- Insert a wooden skewer upright into the hole to form a mast for your car's sail. Secure it at the base with plenty of tape. If it is still too wobbly, you can build a diagonal support out of a piece of cardboard.
- Make at least three sails that are all the same shape but different sizes. For example, for rectangular sails, you could use a whole sheet of paper, a half sheet of paper, and a one-quarter of sheet of paper.
- Now you have a sailcar and sails that are ready to test out!

PROCEDURE

- Poke the upright skewer through both ends of your smallest sail to hold it in place.
- Place your fan on the floor at one end of a long hallway or large room.

- Place your car in front of the fan, and turn the fan on. *How far does your car go before it stops?*
- Replace the smallest sail with your next-biggest sail, and try again. *How far does your car go this time?*
- Try with your largest sail. *Does the car go as far as you expected?*

SCIENCE FAIR IDEA

Try sails that are different shapes. *What shape works the best?*

SCIENCE FAIR IDEA

If you have a variable-speed fan, try the activity on different fan settings. *How does the fan speed affect how far or how fast your car goes?*

OBSERVATIONS AND RESULTS

You might have seen that with the smallest sail, your car started out very slowly. The wind exerts a small force on the small sail, so it may be difficult to overcome friction in the axles so the car can start moving. The car will start more quickly and go farther with a larger sail. There can, however, be diminishing returns with larger sails. Eventually, the extra air the sail can catch does not make up for all the added weight of the sail, so continuing to make the sail bigger will not make the car go any farther.

CLEANUP

Put away the materials you used, and put your sailcar in a safe place.

Train Wheel Science

ALL ABOARD FOR SOME SURPRISING CENTRIFUGAL SCIENCE!

Have you ever watched a train roll by? If so, you might have wondered how the train is able to stay on its tracks. The secret lies in the train's wheels. Although they seem cylindrical at first glance, when looking more closely, you will notice that they have a slightly semi-conical shape. (Of course, never get close to a working train!) This special geometry is what keeps trains on the tracks. In this activity, you will put different wheel shapes to the test to find out why the conical wheel is superior to other designs.

PROJECT TIME

60 to 90 minutes

KEY CONCEPTS

Physics
Engineering
Geometry
Centrifugal force

BACKGROUND

The wheels on each side of a train car are connected with a metal rod called an axle. This axle keeps the two train wheels moving together, both turning at the same speed when the train is moving.

This construction is great for straight tracks. However, when a train needs to go around a bend, the fact that both wheels are always rotating at the same rate can become a problem. The outside of a curve is slightly longer than the inside, so the wheel on the outside rail actually needs to cover more distance than the wheel on the inside rail. You can demonstrate this by drawing a train track—consisting of the two rails—with a turn on a piece of paper. Take a measuring tape (or string and ruler) and measure the length of each line. The outside line of the track should be longer than the inside line. How can one wheel cover more distance than the other one if they both are rotating at the same rate?

This is where the wheels' geometry comes in. To help the wheels stay on the track, their shape is usually slightly conical. This means that the inside of the wheel has a larger circumference than the outside of the wheel. (They also have a flange, or raised edge, on the inner side to prevent the train from falling off the tracks.) When a train with slanted wheels turns, centrifugal force pushes the outside wheel to the larger part of the cone and pushes the inside wheel to the smaller part of the cone. As a result, when a train is turning, it is momentarily running on wheels that are effectively two different sizes. As the outside wheel's circumference becomes larger, it is able to travel a greater distance even though it rotates at the same rate as the smaller inside wheel. The train successfully stays on the tracks! In this activity, you will test for yourself how train wheel shapes impact their ability to stay on track.

MATERIALS

- At least four plastic or Styrofoam cups of the same size (the cups should not have a raised edge at the top)
- Tape
- Two rulers or yardsticks of the same length
- Book or box
- Flat workspace (that can have items taped to it)
- Flexible cardboard or construction paper (optional)
- Scissors (optional)
- Wooden skewers (optional)

PREPARATION

- Take two cups and tape them together with their bases facing each other. This is your first cup setup.
- Take the other two cups and tape them together with their tops facing each other. This is your second cup setup. *Can you describe the differences between the shapes of the first and second cup setup? How do they look similar or different? Which one looks more stable to you?*
- Set up a model railroad track with the two rulers or yardsticks and your book or box. Place the rulers parallel to each other, with one side on the book and the other on the work surface, creating an incline. Stand the rulers up on their sides so that the long narrow sides are pointing up and so you will be able to fit each of the cup setups across the track. Tape the rulers securely in place.

PROCEDURE

- Carefully place the first cup setup across the track at the top of the slope. Try to place it as close to the center as possible. *Why would it matter how you place the cups on the track?*
- Let go of the cup setup, and let it roll down the track. *What do you notice? How does this cup setup behave on the track?*
- Repeat this step several times, and observe what happens to the cup setup on the track each time. *Do you always get the same results?*
- Place the second cup setup onto the tracks. Again, try to place it in the very center of the track.
- Let the cup setup roll down the track. *What happens this time? Are the results similar or different compared to the previous cup setup?*

- Repeat this step several times, and again observe what happens each time. *Do your results change with several attempts, or are they always the same?*
- Take the first cup setup again, and place it on the tracks. This time, place it there off-center. Shift it either slightly to the left or the right. *Do you think this changes your results?*
- Let go of the cup setup, and let it roll down the track. *Does it make it all the way down the tracks without falling off?*
- Take the second cup setup, and place it on the track. Again, place it slightly off-center, either to the left or right. *Do you think it will fall off the tracks?*
- Let the cup setup roll down the track. *What do you observe? Can you explain your observations?*

SCIENCE FAIR IDEA

Use construction paper or cardboard to design other wheel geometries. For example, try a cylindrical shape. *How does this design compare to the others?*

SCIENCE FAIR IDEA

Build a track with an actual turn in it. You can use cardboard or construction paper to do that. Make sure that your track has an incline so you can let your different designs roll down the track. *How do your different designs cope with the turn?*

SCIENCE FAIR IDEA

Instead of taping the two cups together, make wheels that are connected together by a fixed axle as they are in real train wheels. You can use a wooden skewer or another straight rod as the axle. Then, repeat the activity as described above. *Do your results change or stay the same?*

OBSERVATIONS AND RESULTS

The different cup setups represent different train wheel shape possibilities. Both cup setups represent a set of slanted train wheels, but the direction in which the wheels are slanted was exactly the opposite. Whereas in the first setup the outer side of the wheel had the larger diameter, it was the reverse in the second cup setup. The wheel design makes a huge difference in how the wheels behave on a track, as you likely observed.

It was probably difficult to keep the first cup assembly on the track. It should have derailed almost every time before it reached the end of the track. No matter how you placed the cups, they probably fell off the track. This assembly only stays on the track if it is perfectly centered. However, this is almost impossible to accomplish. As soon as the setup is slightly off-center, it will derail on its way down the slope. If you moved the assembly to the left, the part of the cup that was sitting on the left rail had a smaller circumference than the part of the cup that was sitting on the right rail. Thus, the left wheel of the train was smaller than the right wheel of the train. As a result, the whole assembly probably turned even farther to the left—in the direction of the smaller circumference wheel—and eventually fell off the tracks. The opposite was probably the case if you moved the assembly to the right.

The second setup, however, should have stayed on the track—even if you shifted it off-center. When you moved this setup to the left, the part of the cup that was sitting on the left rail became larger than the part of the cup that was sitting on the right rail. In this case, the left wheel of the train was larger than the right wheel of the train. As a result, the assembly probably turned right and corrected its position closer to the center of the track. Whenever this wheel setup became off-centered, it automatically corrected its course toward the center, which makes it a very stable system.

This same principle you observed on the incline also helps the wheels stay on the track when a train is turning. As the wheel sizes change when the train is pushed sideways during a turn, the outside wheel (which becomes larger) is able to move a greater distance than the inside wheel (which becomes smaller). This way, the outside wheel can cover more distance while rotating at the same rate.

CLEANUP

Put away the materials you used.

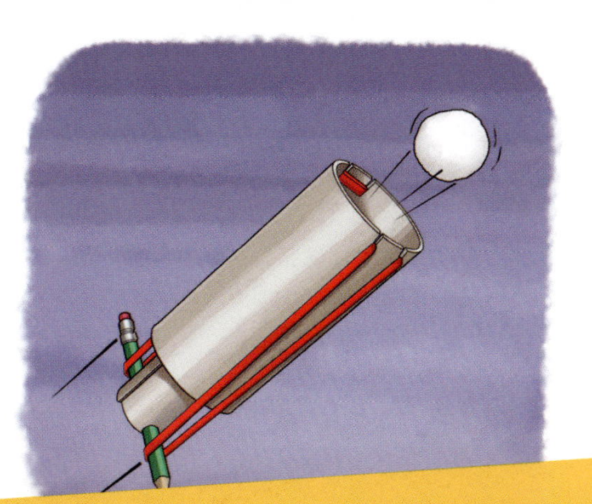

Ready ... Aim ... Energize!

Make Your Own Cotton-Ball Launcher

BLAST OFF—WITH A LITTLE PHYSICS!

PROJECT TIME

60 to 90 minutes

KEY CONCEPTS

Physics
Potential energy
Kinetic energy
Conservation of energy

Have you ever stretched a rubber band and launched it? Put that energy to use, and build a cotton ball launcher in this fun activity!

BACKGROUND

When you stretch a rubber band, it stores elastic potential energy—the energy stored inside a material when it is stretched, squished, bent, or twisted. This is different from gravitational potential energy, which is stored in an object that is lifted off the ground. Both types of potential energy can be converted to kinetic—the energy of motion. All moving objects have kinetic energy, but motionless ones have none. When energy is converted between forms, the total amount of energy remains the same. In other words, it is conserved. (Some energy, however, may also be converted to heat due to friction—but that is still a form of energy.)

In this activity, you'll explore conservation of potential and kinetic energy by measuring the distances you can launch a cotton ball using your own homemade launcher!

MATERIALS

- Short pencil or craft stick
- Two thin rubber bands
- Two empty toilet paper tubes or one empty paper towel tube cut in half
- Packing tape or other strong tape
- Scissors
- Cotton balls
- Yardstick
- Ruler
- Three pieces of paper
- Partner
- Single-hole puncher (optional)

PREPARATION

- Gather your materials in a clear, open area.
- Use your yardstick to measure out a distance of three yards using a piece of paper to mark each yard. Place your yardstick in the first yard. This will be your launching station. *How far do you think you will be able to launch your cotton balls?*

- Use your scissors to carefully cut one of the toilet paper tubes in half lengthwise.
- Squeeze the roll so it becomes narrower (about half the original diameter), and then tape it to hold it in place.
- Use your scissors or your hole puncher to make two holes in the skinny tube. (If you're using a craft stick, use scissors to make narrower holes the same shape as the craft stick.) Make the holes opposite each other, 0.5 inch (1.3 cm) away from the end, so you can poke your pencil or craft stick all the way through the tube.
- Carefully push your pencil or craft stick through the holes.
- On your second toilet paper tube, cut two slits into one end of the tube about 0.25 inch (0.6 cm) long and 0.5 inch (1.3 cm) apart.
- Cut two more slits on the same end of the tube, directly across from the first two.
- Carefully loop one rubber band through the slits on one side so that it hangs from the cardboard piece in the middle. Put a piece of tape over the slits to reinforce the cardboard tab.
- Loop the other rubber band through the slits on the other side of the tube. When you are finished, the tube should have a rubber band hanging from each side.
- Holding the tube so its rubber bands are at the top, slide the narrower tube into the wider one with the pencil end at the bottom.
- Carefully loop each rubber band end around the pencil.
- Hold your launcher so that the pencil is at the bottom. Place a cotton ball on the top so that it rests inside on the narrower tube.

PROCEDURE

- Go to your launching station, and stand next to the zero-end of the yardstick. *Now that you have built your launcher, how far do you think your cotton ball will fly?*
- Hold your launcher slightly horizontally (without dropping the cotton ball). Have your partner hold the ruler next to your launcher.
- Pull back on the pencil so the inner tube extends 2 inches (5 cm) out the back of the launcher. Carefully aim your cotton ball (away from people).
- Release the pencil, and watch your cotton ball fly!
- Use your yardstick to measure the distance the cotton ball traveled.
- Repeat the previous steps, each time pulling the launcher back 1 inch (2.5 cm) farther. *When did the cotton ball travel the shortest distance? When did it travel the farthest?*

SCIENCE FAIR IDEA

Try testing different rubber-band thicknesses, and see which launch the farthest!

OBSERVATIONS AND RESULTS

In this activity, you used two types of energy to load and launch your cotton ball. As you drew back on the pencil with the cotton ball loaded, you were adding potential energy to the system. The farther you pulled back on the pencil, the more potential energy was being stored. When you released the pencil, the energy became kinetic, and the cotton ball should have gone flying through the air!

The farther you pulled back on your launcher, the more potential energy you added to the system—and the more you stored, the more kinetic energy should have been released when you shot the cotton ball. As a result, the farther you pulled back on the launcher, the farther the cotton ball should have traveled.

CLEANUP

Put away the materials you used.

Make a Toy Sailboat

FLIP OR FLOAT? BUILD A TINY BOAT THAT CAN REALLY SET SAIL—WITH THE HELP OF A LITTLE PHYSICS.

It's time to set sail! Even if you don't live near a lake or ocean, you will get to do some sailing in this science activity as you build your own toy sailboat. However, first you have to make sure your boat doesn't capsize! Are you up for the challenge?

PROJECT TIME

30 to 60 minutes

KEY CONCEPTS

Physics
Forces
Weight
Buoyancy
Gravity
Center of mass

BACKGROUND

Do you remember playing with toy boats in the bathtub—or have you ever been on a real boat? Boats can float because of buoyancy. At the same time that they are pulled down by the force of their own weight (caused by gravity), they are pushed up by the buoyant force, which is equal to the weight of the volume of water they displace. Some boats are made of materials that are less dense than water, meaning they have less mass per unit volume. These materials will always float. Other boats, however, are made of metals such as steel, which are much denser than water. So how do they float? They can float because they're hollow, so there is a lot of empty air space inside the boat's hull. The average density of the boat (including both the metal and the air) is lower than the density of water.

Boats don't just need to float—they also need to stay upright and avoid capsizing, or flipping over. To do this, they need a low center of mass, meaning their weight is concentrated toward the bottom of the boat, not the top. That might seem like it would be a problem for sailboats, which have very tall sails that stick way up into the air. How do they stay balanced with so much mass concentrated way up high? They do so with another part called the keel, which is on the bottom of the boat. (If you've only ever seen a sailboat from above the water, you might not even know the keel existed!) The keel is a big part under the boat, shaped like a fin, which serves two purposes. It holds the ballast, or heavy weight, that helps lower the boat's center of mass. It also helps prevent the boat from being blown sideways by the wind. In this project you'll see how a keel can help keep a sailboat from flipping over and help it go straight.

MATERIALS

- Three wine corks
- Two rubber bands
- Toothpick
- Several screws or nails
- Waterproof material, such as craft foam, wax paper, or a paper milk carton, to make a sail
- Aluminum foil
- Sink, bathtub, or large container you can fill with water (The container should be deeper than the length of your nails/screws.)

PREPARATION

- Fill your container with water. Make sure the water is deep enough so you can vertically submerge your longest nail/screw.

PROCEDURE

- Line up three corks (side by side, not end to end).
- Use two rubber bands to hold the corks together, forming a "raft."
- Poke a toothpick into the center cork so it sticks straight up. This is your boat's mast (the part that holds the sail).
- Cut a square of your thin waterproof material to make a sail. It should be about 2.5 inches (6 cm) across.
- Poke the toothpick through opposite ends of the sail (near the edges) to hold it in place.
- You've made your first sailboat! Put it in the water. *What happens?*
- Blow on the sail from behind. *What happens?*
- Now make a skinnier boat by removing the rubber bands and the two outer corks. Keep the sail in place. Depending on how you attached the sail initially, you might need to rotate it 90 degrees.
- Put your new sailboat back in the water. *What happens?*
- Uh-oh! Your sailboat probably tipped over! That's not good. To fix it, try adding a keel. Carefully stick a nail or screw into the bottom of the boat, directly opposite the sail.

- Try putting the boat back in the water. *Does it stay upright this time?*
- If your boat doesn't stay upright, keep adding nails or screws (in a straight line with the first one) until it can float without tipping over.
- Now try blowing on the sail again. *What happens? Does your boat move in a straight line?*
- Right now, your keel is made of one or more nails/screws, but they are not connected to one another. Cut a rectangular piece of aluminum foil, and tightly wrap it around the nails/screws to make a fin shape.
- Put your boat back in the water, and try blowing on the sail again. *What happens this time? Does it go straight?*

SCIENCE FAIR IDEA

Try making a bigger sail and using part of a wooden skewer for the mast instead of a toothpick. *How heavy does your ballast need to be to balance the boat with a bigger sail?* Hint: Try attaching a horizontal nail/screw to the bottom of your keel to act as ballast. That way you don't have to keep poking more nails/screws into the cork.

OBSERVATIONS AND RESULTS

Your first sailboat was probably pretty stable because it was very wide (made from three corks). When you removed two corks to make it skinnier, however, your sailboat probably became unstable and tipped over. It's similar to standing with your feet tightly together instead of spread out slightly—it's harder to balance. When you added nails/screws to the bottom of your sailboat, you lowered its center of mass and made it more stable. Individual vertical nails, however, don't do a very good job of pushing against the water—the water can flow right around them. That means the keel doesn't do a good job making the boat go straight. If you blew on the sail, your boat might have curved off to one side or spun in circles. When you wrapped the nails in aluminum foil, you made the keel more like a fin. It can cut through the water very easily in one direction, but it provides a lot of resistance against the water in the other direction. That makes it easier for your boat to move forward and harder for it to move sideways. This is why real sailboats can be long, skinny, and have tall sails—the keel prevents them from tipping over and helps them go straight!

CLEANUP

Put away the materials you used and clean up any water that may have spilled. If you want to keep your sailboat, put it in a safe place.

Build a Rubber-Band Powered Car

ZOOM! HOW FAST CAN YOU GO WITH PHYSICS? BUILD THIS RUBBER BAND-POWERED CAR, AND FIND OUT!

PROJECT TIME

90 to 120 minutes

KEY CONCEPTS

Physics
Potential energy
Kinetic energy
Conservation of energy
Simple machines

Admit it, you've probably launched a rubber band at least once—pulled one end back and let it go flying. Did you ever suspect that rubber bands could also be a fun way to learn about physics and engineering? Find out in this project where you'll build a rubber band-powered car.

BACKGROUND

When you stretch a rubber band, it stores potential energy. Specifically it stores elastic potential energy—the type of energy stored when a material is deformed (as opposed to gravitational potential energy, the type you get when you raise an object off the ground). When you release it all, that stored energy has to go somewhere. If you launch a rubber band across the room, the potential energy is converted to kinetic energy, the energy of motion.

However, what about putting all that stored energy to use? You can attach your rubber band to a simple machine—a wheel and axle—to build a simple rubber band-powered car. In real cars, gasoline's chemical energy or the electrical energy in a battery is converted to kinetic energy of the moving car. Your model car will use a rubber band as the source of energy. It will take a little engineering to get your vehicle working—challenge yourself to see how far your car can go!

MATERIALS

- Corrugated cardboard
- Two drinking straws
- Two wooden skewers
- Four CDs (that are okay to get scratched)
- Sponge
- Paper clip
- Assorted rubber bands
- Tape
- Scissors
- Flat, hard surface for testing your car
- Hot-glue gun (optional)

Note:
This is an engineering design project. The above list is a suggested list of materials, but you can substitute different ones.

PREPARATION

- Carefully cut a piece of corrugated cardboard that is slightly longer and wider than the length of one straw.
- Tape the two straws to the cardboard, parallel to each other, one at each end.
- Cut a rectangular notch in the cardboard on one end, about 1 inch by 1 inch (2.5 cm by 2.5 cm). This will also cut a segment out of the middle of one of the straws.
- Insert a wooden skewer through each straw. These will be your car's axles.
- Cut four small squares from the sponge and carefully press them onto the ends of the skewers.
- Attach CDs to the axles to form wheels. Do this by stuffing a piece of sponge into the hole in the middle of the CD, then using tape to secure the CD and prevent it from wobbling.
- Make sure your car can roll smoothly. Put it down on a flat surface, and give it a push. If necessary, adjust the wheels so they are all parallel and don't wobble. *How far do you think your car will go when you power it with elastic rubber band energy?*

PROCEDURE

- Loop a rubber band through itself around the middle, exposed part of the wooden skewer (where you cut out a notch in the cardboard and straw).
- Tape the rubber band to the skewer to prevent it from slipping—when the skewer rotates, the rubber band should rotate with it.
- Cut a small slot in the middle of the piece of cardboard.

- Hook a paper clip through the slot.
- Hook the free end of the rubber band onto the paper clip.
- Wind up the axle that's connected to the rubber band. If necessary, pinch the rubber band on the axle when you start to prevent it from slipping.
- Put your car down, and release the axle. *What happens? Does your car move forward? How far does it go?*
- If your car didn't move, it's time for some troubleshooting:
    - If the rubber band didn't unwind at all, wind it more tightly, and try again. You can also try changing the location of the slot for the paper clip to adjust the rubber band's tightness.
    - If the rubber band unwound but the axle didn't spin, then the rubber band might not have been attached securely enough to the skewer. Try attaching it to the skewer by tying a tight knot or using hot glue.
    - If the wheels spun but the car didn't move forward at all, there might not have been enough friction between the CDs and the ground. Try using the car on a different surface. If that still doesn't work, try giving your CDs more grip by stretching rubber bands around them or by putting a bead of hot glue along the edges. (Let the glue dry completely before you test your car again.)
- Keep experimenting with your car. Make small changes to it and test it again. *How far can you get the car to go?*

SCIENCE FAIR IDEA

Think of the "fuel economy" for your rubber band-powered car. Gasoline-powered cars calculate their fuel economy in miles per gallon, or how many miles the car can travel on one gallon of fuel. Your car uses a stretched rubber band as the energy source instead of gasoline. *How could you measure the "fuel economy" for different designs? For example, how many feet can your car travel per initial windup rotation of the axle? How does this change with different rubber bands or different paper clip positions? What gives you the best fuel economy?*

SCIENCE FAIR IDEA

Test different types of rubber bands to power your car. *Does it work better with long or short ones? Thick or thin ones?*

SCIENCE FAIR IDEA

Try using different materials to build your car. *What happens if you use bottle caps instead of CDs for wheels or pencils instead of skewers for axles?*

SCIENCE FAIR IDEA

Do this project with friends or family. Everyone can build their own car and then see whose can go the farthest.

SCIENCE FAIR IDEA

You can build a car powered by a balloon instead of a rubber band. See page 49 for instructions.

OBSERVATIONS AND RESULTS

When you wind up the car's axle, you stretch the rubber band and store potential energy. When you release it, the rubber band starts to unwind, and the potential energy is converted to kinetic energy as the car is propelled forward. The more you stretch the rubber band, the more potential energy is stored, and the farther and faster the car should go.

That all sounds great in theory—but in practice, you might have found it difficult. Several things can prevent your car from working well. If the wheels are not aligned properly, they can wobble or jam and prevent the car from rolling smoothly. The rubber band can slip relative to the wooden axle, preventing the wheels from spinning. Even if the wheels do spin, there might not be enough friction with the ground, causing them to spin in place without moving the car. These are all challenges you can overcome with a little engineering effort!

CLEANUP

Put away the materials you used. Throw out or recycle any scraps.

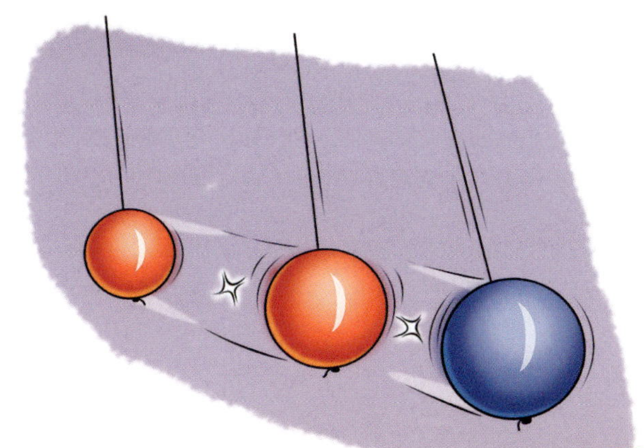

Make a Toy Built for Collisions

TRY THIS WHIZ-BANG ACTIVITY FOR YOURSELF—AND DISCOVER THE POWER OF MOMENTUM!

Did it ever occur to you that tennis, bowling, and shopping carts bumping into each other all involve collisions? It is fascinating how just a few rules of physics can predict the outcome of these collisions. You can discover these rules yourself with a fun homemade toy. After creating and playing with the toys in this activity, you will be one step closer to understanding what happens when you hit a tennis ball or go bowling!

PROJECT TIME

60 to 75 minutes

KEY CONCEPTS

Physics
Collision
Momentum
Energy

BACKGROUND

Have you ever heard someone say that something "has a lot of momentum"? In everyday language, we use "a lot of momentum" to describe things that are hard to stop. In physics, an object's momentum depends on its speed—how fast it moves—and its mass—how much stuff it is made of. Momentum also has a direction—the same direction the object is moving. For an object to gain momentum, it can gain speed, gain mass, or gain both. To give a shopping cart rolling downhill more momentum, you can make it move faster (increase its speed), load more weight (increase its mass), or do both. You probably intuitively know that the shopping cart with the biggest momentum—the fast-moving, heavily loaded cart—is hardest to stop. It also creates the biggest impact when colliding with something.

Physicists discovered that objects transfer momentum when they collide. However, they also observed that the total momentum is conserved during a collision. If you have seen a row of shopping carts creeping away after a fast-moving but empty shopping cart collided into them, you have witnessed conservation of momentum. The fast-moving light cart transferred its momentum to the much heavier row of carts. Its momentum could only make this heavy mass move a little. There is a little more math involved when both objects are moving before the collision, but even then the total momentum is always conserved.

Energy is the other quantity that gets transferred during collisions. More surprisingly, the energy associated with the movement of the colliding objects is conserved in collisions—at least in collisions when the colliding objects do not deform, crack, or break at all. In real life, there is almost always some deformation, and some energy of movement will almost always be converted into other types of energy, such as heat or sound. The fun toy created in this activity will help you get an intuitive feeling for how momentum and energy are conserved during collisions.

MATERIALS

- Two identical balls, 0.5 inch (1.3 cm) to 3 inches (7.6 cm) in diameter (large round wooden beads, ping-pong balls, small bouncy balls, and round erasers work well)
- At least one more ball the same size, but of a different mass (this ball needs to be at least three times as heavy or three times as light as the identical balls)
- Needle and thimble or strong glue

- Thick thread (preferably not twine but a slightly thicker sturdy thread)
- Scissors
- Ruler

PREPARATION

- Cut the thread into pieces about 1 foot (30 cm) long (one for each ball).
- If you are using beads, pull the thread through the hole, and make a knot on one end of the thread big enough so the bead cannot slip over it.
- For any balls you are using, ask an adult to help you hang the balls on threads. Ask them to pierce a threaded needle through the middle of the ball. Make sure they wear a thimble. If needed, pliers can help pull the needle through. Make a knot on one end of the thread so the ball can't fall off. If this is too hard, strong glue can be used to attach a thread to the balls.

PROCEDURE

- Pinch the threads of the two identical balls (or beads) between your thumb and finger, letting the balls hang down. Slide the thread of one ball up or down until the balls are level.
- Pull one ball up 90 degrees, keeping its thread taut so it forms a horizontal line.
- Keep the hand holding the threads steady while you release the ball, and observe what happens. Repeat the test a few times. *What happens (almost) every time?*

- For the second test, go through the same procedure, only now jerk the hand holding the threads up about 1 inch (2.5 cm) each time the balls move away from each other. Move the hand back down when the balls approach each other. You might need to try it a few times before you can keep the balls bouncing. *How is this different from the first test? Why would this be the case?*
- *What do you think will happen if you switch one ball with a heavier or lighter ball?*
- Hold the threads of two non-identical balls between your thumb and finger. Repeat the first test. First, try releasing the lighter ball and observe, then switch to the heavier ball. *How is this similar and how is it different from what you observed when using identical balls?*
- Keep the threads of the non-identical balls pinched between your fingers, and try the second test. *What do you observe now? Can you explain your observations?*
- *Was your prediction correct?*
- To turn your tests into a toy, first select the combination of balls you like best. Then, knot the thread ends farthest from the balls together. Before you tighten the knot, adjust the distances between the knot and the balls so these are identical.

SCIENCE FAIR IDEA

Test different combinations of balls. *What can we learn from a test using same-size balls of different masses? What about balls of equal mass but different sizes?*

SCIENCE FAIR IDEA

Test the role of the material of the balls. *What happens if you use two wooden balls instead of two rubber balls or two ping-pong balls? Which balls keep bouncing the longest if you keep your hand still? Which ones do you have to jerk more to keep them bouncing? Why would this be the case?*

SCIENCE FAIR IDEA

If you have more identical small balls (e.g. marbles), you can do another surprising collision test. Place a row of the balls in a crease of an opened book. All balls should touch each other. Softly shoot a ball along the crease into the end of the row of balls and observe what happens. *Why would this happen? Is it different if you shoot two balls into the other balls, or if you shoot a heavier ball into the row of balls?*

OBSERVATIONS AND RESULTS

When you tried this activity with the identical balls, did you witness the balls exchange speed during the collision? Did you see how jerking the system up makes it possible to keep the balls bouncing? When you tried with non-identical balls, did you notice that the collision didn't cause the heavier ball to move as much while the lighter ball was launched off a high speed?

When two balls collide, they exchange momentum. For identical balls, this means one ball is launched off with the speed of the other ball each time they collide. This explains why the initially motionless ball shot off when bumped by another ball, leaving the first ball almost motionless. Before long, the ball that was shot off returned and bumped into the first, which shot off, returned, and so on.

If the second ball shoots off with the same speed, that ball should shoot up to the same height from which you released the first ball. Was that what you observed? Probably not! With each collision, some energy goes into moving the tiny particles that make up the balls or particles in the air. We observe this as energy of motion being transformed into heat or sound. As a result, the second ball shoots off with a smaller speed than the speed at which it was hit. The difference depends on the material of your balls. Bouncy balls will show a small difference; the speed will decrease only slightly with each collision, and the balls bounce back and forth for a long time. Wooden balls will have a bigger difference and bounce back and forth only a few times before all energy is transformed into heat or sound. Did you notice that when you jerked the system up just after the collision, the balls could keep on going? By doing so, you added energy back into the system, allowing the balls to keep bouncing.

Non-identical balls also exchange momentum, but if their masses are different, there is more to it than a simple exchange of speed. Did you notice how the motion of the lighter ball was only able to make the heavier ball creep up a little bit? On the other hand, when the heavier ball bumped into the lighter ball, its momentum could make the lighter ball move a lot. This is because the same momentum can make a lighter ball move much faster than a heavy ball.

CLEANUP

Put away the materials you used.
Put your new toy in a safe place.

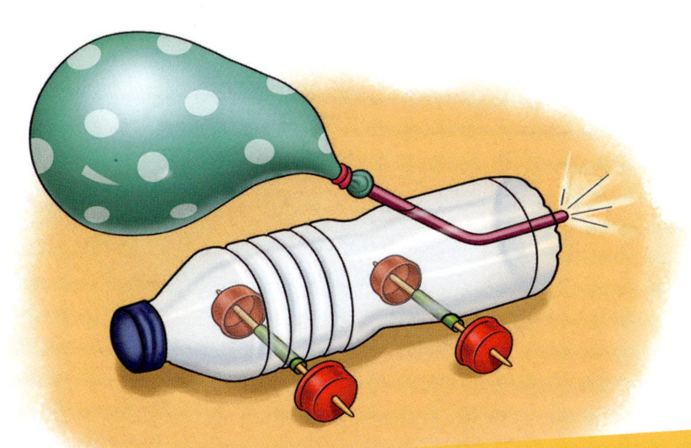

Build a Balloon-Powered Car

START YOUR (BALLOON) ENGINES! LEARN HOW YOU CAN POWER A TOY CAR WITH AIR—AND A LITTLE KNOWLEDGE OF PHYSICS. THEN, CHALLENGE A FRIEND TO A RACE!

PROJECT TIME

60 to 90 minutes

KEY CONCEPTS

Physics
Kinetic energy
Potential energy
Conservation of energy
Newton's laws of motion

Turn a pile of trash into a toy car—and watch it go! In this activity, you will learn some physics concepts and use recycled materials to build a toy car that is propelled by a balloon. You can even find a friend, build two cars, and race them against each other. Whose car will go the fastest?

BACKGROUND

It might not seem like it at first, but a simple balloon car is loaded with physics and engineering concepts! When you inflate a balloon, it stores potential energy in the form of stretched rubber and the compressed air inside. When you release the balloon, this energy is converted to kinetic energy—the energy of motion—as the balloon zooms around the room. Some of the energy is also converted to heat due to friction. According to the law of conservation of energy, the total amount of energy is conserved. Energy never "disappears"—it just changes to another form.

Another way to think about the balloon's movement is to use Newton's third law of motion: For every action, there is an equal and opposite reaction. When you inflate a balloon and then release the nozzle, the rubber contracts and pushes the air out the nozzle. This means that there must be an equal and opposite reaction—the air pushes back on the rubber, propelling the balloon forward. This principle is used in real rockets and jets that shoot a high-speed stream of gases out the back of their engines, propelling the vehicle forward. In this project, you will use this principle to build a toy car that is propelled forward by the stream of air escaping a balloon as it deflates.

The car also contains a simple machine: the wheel and axle. This invention has been around so long, we take it for granted—and many of us ride in wheeled vehicles every day. You will see, however, that getting your wheel and axle to spin smoothly is a critical part of getting your balloon car to work!

MATERIALS

- Plastic bottle
- Four plastic bottle caps
- Wooden skewer
- Two straws
- Balloon
- Tape
- Scissors or sharp knife (Have an adult use or supervise your use of this tool.)
- An adult helper

PREPARATION

- Cut one of the straws in half.
- Tape both pieces of the straw to one side of the water bottle.

- Cut the wooden skewer in half, and push each piece through one of the straws. These will form your axles. (Have an adult help.)
- Have an adult help use the scissors to poke a "+"-shaped hole directly in the center of each plastic bottle cap.
- Press each bottle cap onto the ends of the wooden skewers. These will form your wheels.

PROCEDURE

- Put your car down on a flat surface, and give it a good push. Make sure the car rolls easily and coasts for a bit before stopping. If your car gets stuck or does not roll smoothly, make sure your axles are parallel to each other; the hole in each bottle cap is centered; and the straws are securely taped to the water bottle and do not wobble. You can add some glue if tape is not sufficient.
- Tape the neck of the balloon around one end of the other straw. Wrap the tape very tightly so the connection is airtight.
- Cut a small hole in the top of the water bottle, just big enough to push the straw through.
- Push the free end of the straw through the hole and out the mouth of the bottle.
- Use tape to secure the straw to the bottle.
- Blow through the straw to inflate the balloon, then put your finger over the tip of the straw to trap the air. *What do you think will happen when you put the car down and release your finger?*
- Put the car down on a flat surface, and release your finger. *What happens?*

- See what adjustments you can make to make the car go farther.
- *What happens if you inflate the balloon more?*
- *What happens if you adjust the direction the straw is aimed? Does it work best if the straw is aimed straight back?*

SCIENCE FAIR IDEA

There are many different ways to build a balloon car. Turn this into an engineering design project and try building your car with different materials. For example: *What happens if you use a cardboard box instead of a plastic bottle for the body? What happens if you use different diameter straws? What about different materials for the wheels and axles?* Get some friends and try building different cars and racing them against one another. *What materials work the best?*

OBSERVATIONS AND RESULTS

When you inflate a balloon and let it go, it zips randomly around the room. When you tape the balloon to a straw and attach it to the body of your car, however, you can control the direction of the escaping air. When the end of the straw is aimed backward, the air pushes your car forward, as described by Newton's third law of motion. Your design will be most efficient if the straw is pointed straight back and not downward or to the side. The more you inflate the balloon, the more potential energy it stores, which in turn is converted to more kinetic energy, according to the law of conservation of energy—so the car will go faster.

You may find your car does not work perfectly on the first try, particularly if its axles are not parallel or the wheels wobble. Too much friction can cause the wheels to get stuck, and the balloon will not be powerful enough to push the car forward. Test your car to make sure the wheels spin freely and, when you give it a push, the car rolls easily. If not, you might need to make some adjustments to your design. You should also make sure no air escapes the balloon where it is taped to the straw, and re-tape it more tightly if necessary.

CLEANUP

Put away the materials you used.

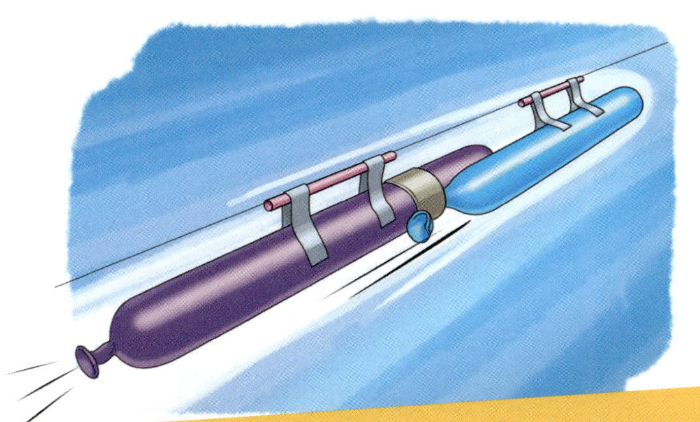

Build a 2-Stage Balloon Rocket

3...2...1... BLAST OFF! TRY YOUR HAND AT MAKING A BALLOON ROCKET THAT HAS TWO BOOSTERS, AND LEARN HOW MUCH THIS CAN HELP IN GETTING REAL ROCKETS INTO SPACE.

If you have ever watched a rocket launch on TV, you might have noticed that rockets have multiple stages. Some parts of the rocket fall off and burn up in the atmosphere, whereas the rest of the rocket keeps going. Why does this happen? Try this activity to find out and build your own two-stage rocket using balloons!

PROJECT TIME

90 to 120 minutes

KEY CONCEPTS

Physics
Energy
Newton's laws
Spaceflight

BACKGROUND

Imagine you are carrying a heavy backpack while hiking up a mountain. That takes a lot of energy, right? Now imagine you want to hike all the way to the mountaintop so you can see the nice view—but when you are halfway through your hike, you decide to leave your backpack so you don't have to carry it all the way to the top. That means the second half of your hike won't require as much energy as the first half.

The same concept applies to launching rockets. It takes a great amount of energy to send things into space. Rather than building a single, huge rocket that goes all the way into orbit, scientists and engineers have developed multistage rockets. When the first stage is done burning its fuel, it breaks away and falls back to Earth. This allows the smaller, lighter second stage of the rocket to keep going, without carrying the weight of the first stage. This approach requires less fuel overall to boost something into orbit.

In this project, you will build your own two-stage rocket with balloons. When you inflate a balloon and then release the nozzle, air is pushed out the back of the balloon. According to Newton's third law of motion (for every action, there is an equal and opposite reaction), this means the balloon will be pushed forward. This allows you to make a simple (and safe!) rocket with some common household supplies.

MATERIALS

- Two modeling balloons (These are the long, skinny kind used to make balloon animals, not the round kind.)
- Two straws
- Two large binder clips
- Paper towel tube
- Fishing line or string (A fishing line will generally work better because it has lower friction.)
- Scissors
- Clear or masking tape
- One other person to help set up the rocket

- Balloon pump, to make it easier to inflate the balloon (optional)
- Two sturdy pieces of furniture at least several feet apart (to which you can tie your fishing line or string)—the farther, the better!
- Open space where you can set up the activity

PREPARATION

- Fishing line can be hard to see—make sure you warn other people that you are doing this project so they don't walk into the line.
- Thread the fishing line through the two straws.
- Tie the ends of the fishing line to two sturdy pieces of furniture and make sure it is pulled tight. The longer you can make the line, the better.
- Cut a small ring (less than 1 inch, or 2.5 cm, in diameter) from the cardboard tube.
- Stretch the balloons to loosen them before inflating

PROCEDURE

- Inflate the first balloon about three-quarters full. Have your helper pinch the balloon's nozzle shut, but do not tie it. Optionally, you can use a binder clip to pinch the nozzle and prevent the balloon from deflating.
- Pull the first balloon's nozzle through the cardboard ring and press it up against the side. Make sure you do not let the balloon deflate.

- Thread the second balloon partially through the cardboard ring, so its nozzle is facing the same direction as the first balloon.
- Carefully inflate the second balloon about three-quarters full. Your goal is to inflate the balloon such that it presses up against the inside of the cardboard ring and squeezes the nozzle of the first balloon shut. This can take some practice—be patient! It will be much easier if you have one person hold on to the cardboard ring and the first balloon while another person inflates the second balloon. If you do this perfectly, you should be able to release the nozzle of the first balloon without deflating it. If you have trouble, you can keep the first balloon's nozzle pinched shut for now.
- Keep the nozzle of the second balloon pinched shut, either with your fingers or a binder clip.
- Tape the balloons to the drinking straws, with the balloons pointing along the fishing line. Do your best to make sure the balloons and straws are in a straight line. If the balloons are very curved and the straws are twisted at an angle, this will cause extra friction along the fishing line and slow your rocket down.
- *What do you think is going to happen when you release your balloons?*
- Pull the balloons to one end of the line, and release both nozzles. *What happened? How are your two balloons similar to the two stages of a rocket? How much farther did your two-stage rocket go than it would have gone if you had had just one balloon?*

SCIENCE FAIR IDEA

Try adding additional balloons to make a three- (or more) stage rocket.

SCIENCE FAIR IDEA

Try tying your string vertically instead of horizontally. *How high can you get your rocket to go?*

SCIENCE FAIR IDEA

Do a test to compare different types of rockets. *What happens if you compare a two-stage rocket like the one you built to a single rocket with two balloons next to each other that deflate at the same time? Can one type go farther than the other?*

OBSERVATIONS AND RESULTS

You should have observed that your two balloons behave like the two stages of a rocket. One balloon keeps the other balloon's nozzle pinched shut at first, preventing them both from deflating at the same time. So, that balloon deflates first—acting like the first stage of the rocket and pushing both balloons along the string. After it has deflated, the second balloon's nozzle is released, and it acts like the second stage of the rocket—continuing to move along the string while leaving the first balloon behind (as long as you didn't tape them together). Ideally, this should allow the second balloon to travel farther than it could if it had to continue dragging along the weight of the first one.

As noted above, however, this can take some practice to get right. It can be difficult to get one balloon to pinch the other balloon's nozzle shut perfectly. You might accidentally have both balloons deflate at the same time. If this happens, don't get frustrated! Just like a real engineer, you can learn from your mistakes and try again. After a couple tries, especially if you have someone else to help keep the balloons pinched shut, you should be able to get your rocket working.

CLEANUP

Take down your fishing line as soon as you are finished with the activity; reuse other materials as possible or throw away.

THE SCIENTIFIC METHOD

The scientific method helps scientists—and students—gather facts to prove whether an idea is true. Using this method, scientists come up with ideas and then test those ideas by observing facts and drawing conclusions. You can use the scientific method to develop and test your own ideas!

Question: What do you want to learn? What problem needs to be solved? Be as specific as possible.

Research: Learn more about your topic, and refine your question.

Hypothesis: Form an educated guess about what you think will answer your question. This allows you to make a prediction you can test.

Experiment: Create a test to learn if your hypothesis is correct. Limit the number of variables, or elements of the experiment that could change.

Analysis: Record your observations about the progress and results of your experiment. Then, analyze your data to understand what it means.

Conclusion: Review all your data. Did the results of the experiment match the prediction? If so, your hypothesis was correct. If not, your hypothesis may need to be changed.

GLOSSARY

buoyancy: The power of rising and floating, or the power of a liquid to hold up a floating body.

centrifugal: Moving away from a center or axis.

conical: Shaped like a cone.

corrugated: Having a wavy surface.

diameter: A straight line that runs from one side of a figure and passes through the center.

diminishing returns: The idea that as more input is applied to something, the output decreases.

displace: To move physically out of position.

engineering: The application of science to the goal of creating useful machines or structures.

fuel economy: The distance a car can travel using a certain amount of fuel.

geometry: A branch of mathematics that deals with points, lines, angles, surfaces, and solids.

insulation: Material that is used to stop the passage of electricity, heat, or sound from one conductor to another.

nozzle: On a balloon, the pinched area that allows air to flow in or out.

physics: A science that deals with the facts about matter and motion and includes the subjects of mechanics, heat, light, electricity, sound, and the atomic nucleus.

propulsion: The force that moves something forward.

prototype: An original or first model of something from which other forms are copied.

skewer: A piece of wood or metal, often used for fastening meat to keep it in form while roasting or to hold small pieces of meat or vegetables for broiling.

ADDITIONAL RESOURCES

Books

Canavan, Roger. *The Science of Vehicles*. Brighton, UK: Book House, 2019.

Rader, Andrew, and Galen Frazer. *Rocket Science: A Beginner's Guide to the Fundamentals of Spaceflight*. Somerville, MA: Candlewick Press, 2020.

Smibert, Angie. *Mind-Blowing Physical Science Activities.* North Mankato, MN: Capstone Press, 2021.

Websites

Exploratorium
https://www.exploratorium.edu/search/science%20fair%20projects

Science Buddies
https://www.sciencebuddies.org/science-fair-projects/project-ideas/list

Science Fair Central
sciencefaircentral.com

Science Fun
https://www.sciencefun.org/?s=science+fair

Videos

"Can You Transform a Toy Car into a Pullback Car?"
https://ny.pbslearningmedia.org/resource/pullback-car-science-u/pullback_car/, PBS Learning Media, 1:38.

"Remotely Operated Vehicles"
https://ny.pbslearningmedia.org/resource/ate10.sci.engin.design.rov/remotely-operated-vehicles/, PBS Learning Media, 3:31.

INDEX